why i travel alone

poems by

joan cappello

Finishing Line Press
Georgetown, Kentucky

why i travel alone

Copyright © 2019 by Joan Cappello
ISBN 978-1-64662-084-5 First Edition
All rights reserved under International and Pan-American Copyright Conventions. No part of this book may be reproduced in any manner whatsoever without written permission from the publisher, except in the case of brief quotations embodied in critical articles and reviews.

ACKNOWLEDGMENTS

Thank you Leah Maines, Christen Kincaid, and the staff of Finishing Line Press.

Thank you Susan Lewis and Bernd Sauermann of *Posit: A Literary Journal* for publishing: "my brief affair," "self esteem," "dream (2)" and "why i travel alone."

Thank you Gregori Maiofis for allowing me to use your fabulous photograph, "Adversity Makes Strange Bedfellows," for the cover of my book.

Thank you John Kramer for your outstanding cover design.

Thank you Kristin and Timmy.

Thank you Roberta Metz Swann, Hettie Jones and Scott Hightower for your interest and guidance.

Thank you Elaine Sexton for your mentorship, friendship, encouragement and boundless generosity. Without it, I literally could not have created this chapbook.

Publisher: Leah Maines
Editor: Christen Kincaid
Cover Art: Gregori Maiofis
Author Photo: Elaine Sexton
Cover Design: John Kramer

Printed in the USA on acid-free paper.
Order online: www.finishinglinepress.com
also available on amazon.com

Author inquiries and mail orders:
Finishing Line Press
P. O. Box 1626
Georgetown, Kentucky 40324
U. S. A.

Table of Contents

why i travel alone 1

little red (night) cap 2

behind enemy lines 3

nothing ever stays put—pantoum blues 4

détaché 5

hey, what's going on here? 6

all i have to do 7

dream (1) 8

dream (2) 9

dream (3) 10

just because i threw-up at your wedding doesn't mean
    i'm still in love with you 11

body language 12

self-esteem 13

72nd street 14

secondary sex characteristics 15

family tree 16

visiting relations 17

neurosis 18

because i believe there has to be someone for everyone ... 19

malocchio vs daytime tv 20

my brief affair 21

last night's dishes 22

white 23

nuclear fission 24

risk! 25

dogs 26

quarrel 27

for
emily and sadie bernstein
elias and aurelia metzger

why i travel alone

your anger erupts red hot, its lava setting fire to the sole of my sandal like that time at the marketplace in lebanon when you called me extravagant for buying too many grapes

little red (night) cap

for a while we sit sipping scotch
watching naked
snaking through

until his opening line

pardon me but are you
one of those women
who run with the wolves
and i say
no i'm just one of those women
who run

then he whispers
i've always had a thing for redheads
as we contemplate
the frayed embroidery cloth
hung over the cash register promising

*you have
the power for greatness*

my room or yours he asks finally
paying for our drinks with bitcoin

and i say yes

behind enemy lines

my father once lived with a stripper
whose thruway turned into a swamp
our car parts tremble and shake
your mechanic checks under the hood

the swamp releases its gases
your parakeets peck the stain off my picture frames
the mechanic complains about work
a woman is wearing your shirt

your parakeets peck the pain off my picture frames
that woman is wearing your shirt
and i am a water buffalo my mother once saw
being swallowed by a snake

nothing ever stays put—pantoum blues

last night you slept in my cactus
this morning all that remains
is the scent of old spice
and sound of neglect

this morning
there's a cat keening under my window
the sound of neglect
and your beauty beyond my control

won't someone please kill that cat?!
i watch tv to think about feeling
and beauty beyond control
pain so fierce it lights up my room

i watch tv—think about feelings
and your aftershave
a pain so fierce it blows-up in my face
last night you slept in my cactus

détaché

trixie our landlady
wants to know
where you've been
the past six months
and why i keep playing
the same marvelettes record
over and over
i pour another glass of sherry
and tell her how
my father's throat became my throat
and that mother was a circle
who turned me into a hologram
and that last august you showed-up
offering a grocery bag full of pillsbury snack cakes
and fistful of wilted violets
then after reciting your ode to paradox
cried "acapulco is a strange place"
and split
so now
i'm storing a bottle of myself
in the pantry
just in case i run out

hey, what's going on here?

the woman i find you kissing sprouts wings then
swoops to peck the top of my head

all i have to do

maya
mother
of buddha
user of veils
i wake-up
stuck
in my dream
obsessing
about the parakeet i spy
in woolworth's window
trapped
flailing
against a mountain of
plastic coolers
and mr. t towels
and my plea for help
to the girl behind the counter
who turns away without a word

when my husband leaves for work
i fall back onto his pillow
to continue my dream
where his left off
unfortunately this one
has to do with
setting fire
to my manuscript

another one of your tricks

maya
i press my ear
to the space between your breasts
and hear nothing

i don't know
maybe there's just not enough god
to go around

dream (1)

you ask what i'm doing
standing naked in front of the medicine cabinet
"looking in the mirror" i say
you leave closing the door quietly behind you

dream (2)

the two of us happy together again on the rue de fleurus
with my crappy french accent
and your odd-ball friends...but this can't be right
i've never been to paris

dream (3)

the audience has questions like how can i
speak with authority with your head in my lap?

**just because i threw-up at your wedding
doesn't mean i'm still in love with you**

you slipped out late last night
with my *new york magazine*
(i was reading that)
leaving me alone
once again
to clean up the chaos

it's too early for lunch
i'm having trouble
finding shoes
that don't hurt my feet

someone phones saying she's from
the katherine gibbs secretarial school
(didn't that place fold years ago)
when she asks for your current address
i tell her to call your wife

late afternoon
spinning lettuce
i catch sight of a raccoon
at the edge of the driveway
drooling into his
little hands
wringing

body language

you may think i'm having another bright
idea but really i'm looking for a way out

self-esteem

i tried to make you think i couldn't be bothered with me
it worked well for you but i soon developed a tic

72nd street

there was a booth at the nickel bar, our booth, where
i'd listen to the juke box and watch you flirt with men

secondary sex characteristics

on my way out the door
in search of rock 'n roll
my father tells me my bra strap is showing
i tell him it's 2019 and nobody cares

in search of rock 'n roll
i find elvis
and let him know it's 2019
sadly he thinks of me as just another fan

i find elvis
at the shallow end of a dirty pool
he thinks i'm just another fan
but i've come to mop up the make-believe

at the shallow end of a dirty pool
elvis presely holds court
i say "i'm here for the make-believe"
he tells me to call harry houdini

because magic is what i need
to prove i'm still alive

family tree

some of my ancestors communicate through tears
is that what you meant when you asked what was wrong?

visiting relations

the uncle with the jolly round face
unzips his pants—it doesn't stop there

neurosis

because i was left alone too long in my cradle
i feel a rocking whenever i leave your bed

because i believe there has to be someone for everyone

of course i remember
we met at gail hanley's barbecue in
white plains

i noticed you immediately
commanding in your london fog
sitting on a director's chair
talking to the hostess through a bullhorn

my hair was a mess

you stole a fondue fork
then we left in a hurry
to make love in your prius
parked at the back of a quarry full of bloodstones

the weekend i came to visit
your shrubs took no interest in me whatsoever
which made your words all the more difficult to swallow
when at the train station
you asked if i wouldn't mind taking your laundry

the last time we met
i believe you were working
from a church basement in astoria
molding communion wafers
out of papier mâché

am i free tonight

let me check

malocchio vs daytime tv

sicilian curse
horn of envy
said to harm sperm
its cosmos opens
and closes
while cousin frankie
sits on the porch
with garlic and lemons
around his neck
hungry for lunch

aunt millie's kitchen
is filled with steam
and revenge
no mea culpas here
only *giustizia*

today i need her
to transport her gaze
from arthur avenue to queens
where my television
has swallowed me
into its vortex of soap opera
i pound the screen
from inside "the young and the restless" crying

i'm in here auntie!

my brief affair

last summer i ran away with an interesting
young man but i was smoking at the time

last night's dishes

we were a mixed metaphor to be sure
me in my blouses from paris
he with his ability to squeeze
the toothpaste back into its tube

so i wasn't surprised
when he ran away with a troupe
of slavic flamenco dancers
after walking in on me
(i knew i should've put
the chain on the door)

i'm so lonely now
and yearn for the opportunity
to not take the advice
my mother would've given
if she were here

in the distance
a car alarm sirens horn-mad
as i dress to join the ladies
waiting in front of *sal's autobody*
for the charter bus
to transport me to a matinee
that no longer involves my husband
coming home for lunch

white

when i am young
i hide my songs
in little white socks
and keep them
like dirty laundry
in a hamper

when i am young
i have a rabbit in my chest
and face full of feeling
in a room with no eyes

when i am young
the virgin mary
sleeps with my teddy bear
then leaves me for jack 'n mac's
on the other side of town

when i am young
(but old enough
to go to the movies)
we buy lipsticks
for twenty-five cents
from a vending machine
in the ladies lounge
where jayne mansfield
waits on line
to use the bathroom

when i am young
a raccoon
sneaks into the house
to steal my masks
then slips them
into the side pockets
of sister mary gerald's
black habit

nuclear fission

when i am rich
i marry a make-believe man
who has a face
like a pin-ball machine

the man i marry
has bushy eyebrows
and writes music
using an electronic bingo cage

the man with the bushy eyebrows
and voice like gunshots
whose birds fly out of control
vaporizes my resistance

and using his voice like gunshots
ignores the periodic table
exploding me into particles
that no longer attach to anything

risk!

the man in the three-piece suit
flicks the ashes of his romeo y julieta cigar
into my souvenir ashtray from asbury park
he asks if i know that birds absorb light
through the tops of their heads
then hands me a feathered cape of good hope
i want to thank him but the room is small
and my voice smaller
besides i can't tell if he's talking about
car parts or carpets—
when i ask if he'd like some casserole
and how do i escape my fate
he says "yes,
you always made such a nice chicken"
then offers to divine my future through eggs
but i'm closer to the ground than he thought
so he opens his book of incarnations
and predicts my move
to a pink cottage
with a steamy pool and
babies in the hen house

dogs

specky, aunt hazel's german shepherd
bit me twice when i was three
then he bit the mailman
and then auntie emma
who died two weeks later
(but not from the bite)

aunt hazel's dog bit me twice
jingles, the saldi's beagle
and aunt emma after she died
chased me home every day after school

despite his shiny name
jingles had sly teeth and a bark
like an old man's cough
that rattled like my auntie's skeleton
dancing on my schoolgirl bed

quarrel

go on do it again. blow my mind!
the impact will be good for me

Joan Cappello's life is a meander, non-linear and open-ended. She has been a backup singer, bank teller, yoga instructor, secretary, film editor, dancer, research assistant, personal assistant, sales assistant, production assistant, mother and grandmother but not necessarily in that order. At this moment she is a massage therapist with a practice in New York City. Her prose and poems have appeared in: *Persimmon Tree, Post Card Poems and Prose Magazine, 2 Horatio* and *Posit: A Literary Journal.*

www.ingramcontent.com/pod-product-compliance
Lightning Source LLC
LaVergne TN
LVHW041514070426
835507LV00012B/1574